BIRMINGHAM AT WORK

Alton & Jo Douglas

© 1993 ALTON and JO DOUGLAS
ISBN 1 85858 014 5
Published by Brewin Books, Doric House, Church Street, Studley, Warwickshire B80 7LG.
Printed in Great Britain
Layout by Alton and Jo Douglas

The Birmingham Small Arms Co. Ltd., Armoury Road, Small Heath, 8th October 1971

Front cover: Assembling "Patrick Specials", Patrick Motors, Bristol Road, Selly Oak, in the thirties.
Title page: Cato Street North, Saltley, 16th October 1956.

CONTENTS

BREWIN BOOKS

Doric House, Church Street
Studley, Warwickshire B80 7LG

Tel: 052 785 4228 Fax: 052 785 2746

VAT Registration No. 378 1070 47

Dear Nostalgic,

You responded so enthusiastically to our most recent book about the city, "Birmingham Shops", that it seemed quite logical to extend the theme and show people in all types of work. Birmingham has been called "The City of 1001 trades" so we've included as many as possible – interesting vocations, professions, callings – anything that means busy people earning a living. As usual you'll also find those entrancing old ads but equally I have to say that I enjoy the inventive slogans, from "Come to Walkers first – it pays in the end" to "Roofers get felt at Moore's Roofing Supplies" to possibly the most famous Birmingham slogan of all, Sword & Robb's………no, I won't quote it, just see if you can remember (the answer lies in one of the photographs in our chapter "At The Centre Of It All").

As I've said before, our books are purely designed for you to enjoy and Jo joins me in sending best wishes to you, with a hope that you'll get hours of pleasure from this, our seventh book about Birmingham – THE City !

Yours, in friendship,

Alton

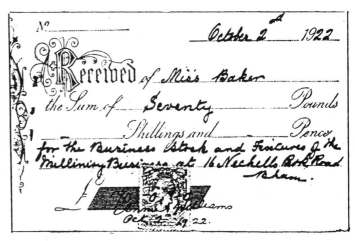

In this fascinating trio of items we see Freda Baker outside her newly-acquired milliner's shop in Nechells Park Road, in 1922, the receipt for the purchase of the shop and then Freda (by now Mrs Dutton) in 1959. The business was known, in time, as The Wool Shop and finally closed in 1968.

3

ADVERTISING SPACE

Hagley Road, Edgbaston, 29th August 1949.

Dale End, with Newton Street on the left, 13th November 1950.

Darwin Street/Leopold Street, Highgate, 8th October 1951

Dudley Street, 8th December 1953

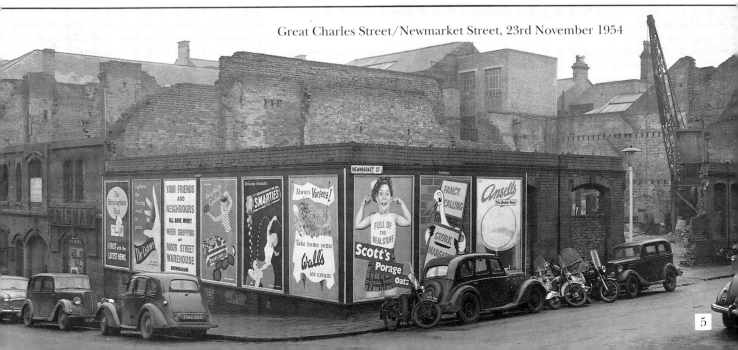

Great Charles Street/Newmarket Street, 23rd November 1954

Alum Rock Road, 10th November 1965

Hobmoor Road, South Yardley, 8th February 1965

1964

FOR YOU AND YOUR FRIENDS
★
MANNEQUIN PARADES
OF
AUTUMN FASHIONS

TUESDAY, 6th September,
11 a.m., 12-30 p.m., 3-0 p.m.

WEDNESDAY, 7th September,
at 11 a.m. only

THURSDAY, 8th September,
11 a.m., 12-30 p.m., 3-0 p.m. and 6-0 p.m.

FRIDAY, 9th September,
11 a.m. and 3-0 p.m.

NORTONS
OF
MOOR STREET
WAREHOUSE

BIRMINGHAM

Telephone: MIDland 2656

Fordhouse Lane, Stirchley, 1st January 1962

AT THE CENTRE OF IT ALL

The buying and selling of horses, outside St Catherine's Church, gave the street its name, Horse Fair, c. 1900

Assembling and packaging smokers' pipes, Singleton & Cole Ltd., Cannon Street, c. 1925.

The staff of the Futurist Cinema get in the mood for "The Volga Boatman", John Bright Street, c. 1928

The announcement by the Minister of Agriculture yesterday that the Government's scheme of fish distribution has been abandoned as a failure is regarded in Birmingham as the end of a disastrous chapter in the history of the fish trade in the city.

A representative of the wholesalers said: "The fish trade in Birmingham managed to supply the public throughout the Great War, a general strike and two railway strikes, but yesterday for the first time in its history in Birmingham, the market had to be closed."

On Tuesday 50 distributing depots under the scheme were entirely without fish and Birmingham was informed early yesterday morning that the whole of the available supplies must go to those centres.

21.9.39

Birmingham Post

WHEN I WAS A LAD I CAME WITH DAD.
NOW I'M A DAD I BRING MY LAD.

CLOTHES
FOR THE LAD
AND HIS DAD!

JAMES PARSONS LTD   SWORD & ROBB   STAN

JAMES
PARSONS
LIMITED

MAURICE
JONES
LADIES' and
CHILDREN'S
UNDERWEAR,
HOSIERY, ETC.

Two-way street to Five Ways soon

21.11.47

IMMEDIATELY official sanction is received from the Ministry of Transport, an important experiment, involving the return to two-way traffic at the Five Ways end of Broad-street, is to be instituted by Birmingham Public Works Department. The change-over, made possible by the cessation of the tram route which used to run across the stream of main road traffic, will involve alterations to both islands at Five Ways and the use of four sets of traffic signals. Official permission is necessary to suspend part of the Five Ways Control Order, which does not actually expire until 1 April next. It is hoped that the new system will result in a considerable speeding up of traffic over what has been a one-way route since 1936. A careful check on the results of the new system will be made by police and City Surveyor's Dept. officials.

One of the best-remembered advertising slogans in
the city! Smallbrook Street, 7th September 1949.

Jackson's Assembly Rooms, Windmill Street/Horse Fair, 29th September 1950.

Corporation Street, 23rd October 1951.

Stephenson Place, 25th November 1953.

Corporation Street, with Lower Priory on the right, 8th October 1953.

Steelhouse Lane, 22nd September 1953.

Birmingham & Midland Institute, Paradise Street, 10th March 1953.

Hill Street/Station Street, 3rd November 1953.

THE BRITISH SCHOOL OF COMMERCE

INCORPORATING LUND'S BUSINESS COLLEGE
PRINCIPAL & PROPRIETOR: N.F. SHEPHERD
CERTIFIED TRANSLATOR OF EUROPEAN LANGUAGES

EDUCATIONAL   SPECIALISTS

TRANSLATIONS · LEGAL
TECHNICAL & COMMERCIAL
ALL EUROPEAN LANGUAGES

PHONE · MIDLAND 0803

HEAD OFFICE
QUEEN'S COLLEGE CHAMBERS
PARADISE STREET
BIRMINGHAM · I

TYPEWRITING · COPYING
DUPLICATING, PRINTING
BY EXPERT STAFF

ESTABLISHED 1874

24th July 1953.

Edgbaston Street, 26th July 1954.

Stock Exchange, Margaret Street, 4th February 1954.

Greys, Bull Street, 28th September 1954.

Corporation Street, with Martineau Street to the left and Union Street on the right, 12th July 1955.

Priory Tea & Coffee Co. Ltd., Lower Priory, c. 1955.

Hurst Street, 25th July 1955.

Queen's Drive, New Street Station, July 1955.

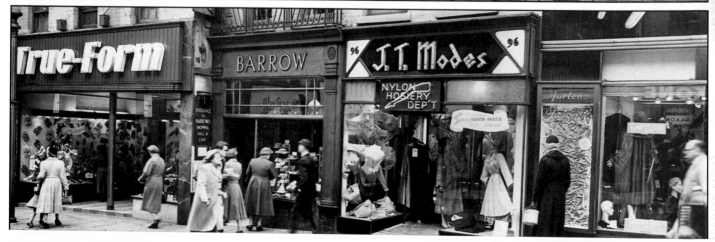

Bull Street, 27th March 1956.

Little Bow Street/Horse
Fair, 4th December 1956

New Street/Corporation Street, 1958.

Corporation Street,
25th September 1956.

Martineau Street, with Union Passage on the right, 5th December 1956.

17

Business as usual for the fish traders, in their new home, formerly the Rag Market, 6th July 1958.

"THE worst Christmas I have ever known" said Len Pillinger from the Bull Ring pitch he'd had for 30 years. The reason — he was having to sell turkeys bought in at 4s. a lb for 3s. 6d.

Hurst Street, looking towards Hill Street,
6th November 1958.

Edmund Street, 8th January 1959.

Hinckley Street, 6th March 1961.

Lionel Street, 30th December 1960.

New Street, 30th November 1960. The Midland Bank building
(with the imposing pillars), re-opened in 1993, as Dillons the Bookstore.

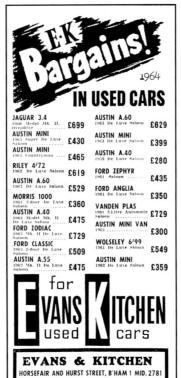
SIXTY sides of fresh beef—a big proportion of all available supplies at Birmingham's Wholesale Market—were sold today to an unknown French buyer.

It was the first sale of its kind in the market's 80-year history, and brought an immediate demand from Mr. Robert Tyler, 38-year-old President of the Birmingham Butchers' Association, for the Government to halt the "meat drain" from Britain.

Mr. Tyler said: "Unless the Government acts to stop this drain on our stock, the British housewife will be completely priced out of the market and meat will be almost a luxury."

1964

Tesco, Bull Ring, 27th April 1967.

17.12.70

ALL Birmingham drivers should put a big red ring round January 3 on their calendars.

That day—the first Sunday in the New Year—will be a red letter day on which a £35,000,000 investment by ratepayers and taxpayers begins to pay real dividends. The Inner Ring Road circling the city centre will then be opened for the first time as a complete traffic route.

NO LONGER WILL IT BE NECESSARY FOR THROUGH TRAFFIC OF ANY KIND TO ENTER THE CITY CENTRE.

And the effect on the city centre could be dramatic, turning some main streets into quiet backwaters outside rush hours.

Birmingham will be the first city in the country, if not in Europe, to have finished a scheme like this of such magnitude.

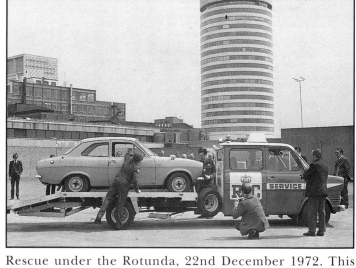

Main line driver, Ken Beasley, gives workers attending the Drivers' Route Training School details of signal devices at New Street Station, 26th May 1971.

Rescue under the Rotunda, 22nd December 1972. This photograph was taken on the day that the RAC changed their logo, after 75 years, to its present form.

Telephone Exchange, Hill Street, 20th August 1973.

King Alfred's Place, 5th March 1976. Today the entrance to the ICC is situated on this site.

A full house as philatelists pack the head post office in Victoria Square for the first issue of Silver Jubilee stamps, 11th May 1977.

BRITISH TELECOM AT RACKHAMS

1981

When Rackhams opened in 1881, the public telephone service in Birmingham was already two years old with about eighty subscribers, and the first telephone directory, issued in 1886, shows an entry for the Cobden Hotel which occupied part of the present Rackhams site. Today Rackhams - one of British Telecoms largest customers in Birmingham - has almost as many exchange lines incorporated in their sophisticated private automatic telephone system as there were original telephone subscribers in Birmingham when the store first opened.

IN STORE

British Telecom are joining Rackhams in their centenary celebrations by providing displays throughout the store, some of which include telephones past, present and future. There will be a sales kiosk in the basement displaying a wide range of British Telecom equipment including attractive up-to-the-minute telephones giving a choice of modern or traditional design styles. One example is the CLASSIC, based on a Victorian - style model: this telephone combines traditional elegance with modern technology to grace any home.

The stagehands assemble the production set for the Hugh Leonard farce, "Some Of My Best Friends Are Husbands", starring Patrick Cargill, Hugh Paddick and Moira Redmond, Alexandra Theatre, 31st May 1976.

Girls from the Priory branch of Lloyds Bank wear red roses, white jumpers and dark skirts to celebrate the opening of their new offices, 31st December 1980.

General foreman, Laurence Dolby, drinks to the success of the Hippodrome as massive renovations come to an end, 2nd September 1981. The theatre re-opened, the following month, with the musical "Jesus Christ, Superstar".

Councillor Najma Hafeez (centre) with the City's first official tourist guides, Chamberlain Square, 26th June 1986.

First World War Recruiting Parade, Corporation Street, 1914.

The uniformed figure of King George V leaving the BSA works, 1917.

William Sapcote & Sons begin laying the foundations for the MEB Power Station in Summer Lane, June 1925.

The construction of the new road begins, British Industries Fair, Castle Bromwich, 1926.

The Prince of Wales (fourth from left) visits the British Industries Fair, 22nd February 1927.

A.J. Gupwell (Shopfitters) Ltd., off for a day in the country, Park Street, Digbeth, 1924.

A SILVER cigarette case, the gift of the sole proprietor, Sir Charles Hyde, recalls the General Strike in May 1926 and the efforts of members of the editorial and commercial staffs to produce *The Birmingham Post* at a time when members of the typographical and other unions were involved in the general stoppage.

Without outside assistance the *Post* gave the public news every day in bulletins and two-page issues totalling 14 columns. Volunteers not engaged in actual production were sworn in as special constables; they kept up a day-and-night patrol of the works and offices.

Each employee who did not go on strike received from Sir Charles Hyde a silver cigarette case inscribed with the words "For Loyalty."

Bournville Girls' Day Continuation School Camp at Central School, Carnavon, 1927.

The team of V. Siviter Smith & Co. Ltd. (commercial photographers), winners of the Birmingham and District Works Amateur Football Association medal competitions, Ludgate Hill, 1937.

Firemen parade in front of a 100 ft turntable ladder, Brigade Display, Calthorpe Park, 1932.

THE GROWTH OF THE CITY COUNCIL

BALLOT BOX

WHEN YOU VOTE—YOU APPOINT THE COUNCILLORS WHO GOVERN THE CITY

1939 MUNICIPAL AIRPORT OPENED
1930 SLUM CLEARANCE CAMPAIGN BEGINS
1930 CITY TAKES OVER PUBLIC ASSISTANCE
1919 BEGINNING OF BIG MUNICIPAL HOUSING SCHEMES
1919 MUNICIPAL ORCHESTRA FOUNDED
1916 MUNICIPAL SAVINGS BANK STARTED
1910 BIRMINGHAM INAUGURATES FIRST TOWN PLANNING SCHEME IN THE COUNTRY
1908 CARE OF MATERNITY AND CHILD WELFARE BEGINS
1904 WELSH WATER SUPPLY COMMENCED
1904 CITY COMMENCED OPERATING THEIR OWN TRAMWAYS
1898 CITY TAKES OVER SUPPLY OF ELECTRICITY
1890 FIRST MUNICIPAL HOUSES
1876 CITY TAKES OVER WATER SUPPLY
1875 CITY FIRE BRIGADE STARTED
1875 CORPORATION STREET CLEARANCE BEGINS WITH IMPROVEMENT SCHEME
1875 CITY TAKES OVER THE SUPPLY OF GAS
1874 FIRST MUNICIPAL HOSPITAL (for fever only)
1872 FIRST MEDICAL OFFICER OF HEALTH APPOINTED
1870 SCHOOL BOARD STARTED
1867 ART GALLERY OPENED
1861 PUBLIC LIBRARY STARTED
1856 ADDERLEY PARK OPENED
1851 THE IMPROVEMENT ACT incorporates powers of old local bodies in Town Council, gives it complete control over roads, sewers, lighting and sanitary arrangements, public buildings, markets and baths.
1850 FIRST CITY ASYLUM AT WINSON GREEN OPENED
1842 ESTABLISHMENT OF POLICE FORCE
1838 THE MUNICIPAL CHARTER INSTITUTES AN ELECTED COUNCIL

When you vote in the Municipal Elections you take your part in electing the Council which, through its Committees, governs the city and manages so many of the services which benefit you. Some of these are self-supporting, and the others are financed from the rates which are levied by the Council on property.

As you can see from this chart, the range of the Council's work has increased enormously since the Council was formed in 1838. It grew very rapidly in 1851 when the Improvement Act was passed, and again in the 1870's in the time of Joseph Chamberlain.

1838 1848 1858 1868 1878 1888 1898 1908 1918 1928 1938

A HUNDRED YEARS OF PROGRESS BRINGS

Ariel "Old-Timers" dinner, 28th June 1945. Ariel Motor Cycles Ltd., were based in Grange Road, Selly Oak.

Wacaden Dairy employees, from Hubert Road depot, Selly Oak, enjoy their
Christmas Party at The Raven, Weoley Castle, c. 1950.

BIRMINGHAM
had built a canvas palace fit for a Queen in the heart of the Welsh mountains.

The Queen was Elizabeth II. The occasion the opening of the giant £2,000,000 Claerwen Dam on October 23, 1952.

It was the Midland's proudest moment of the year — though so far away.

In the marquees deep carpetings covered the rocky earth. The scent of 10,000 blooms filled the air and in the special retiring rooms erected for the Queen and the Duke of Edinburgh there was an atmosphere of palatial luxury.

It was on Whit Monday, May 20, 1872, that two sturdy horses pulled Birmingham's first tramcar from the city boundary at Hockley Brook, up Soho Hill, along Holyhead Road and on to Hill Top, West Bromwich, plodding their way at a steady five miles an hour.

Just over 80 years later the city's last tram, powered by overhead electric cables, rumbled its way out to Erdington and back to the city centre and was feted all the way by cheering crowds.

Lloyds Bank, New Street/Worcester Street, c.1954. The party was to
celebrate the retirement of a senior member of staff.

Sports day at Henry Wiggins & Co. Ltd. (nickel alloys), Ridgacre Road, Quinton, 1956.

Christmas Party, James Booth Aluminium Ltd., Kitts Green Road, Kitts Green, 1959.

The biggest attraction at the Birmetal's Industries' sports day proves to be a helicopter, Woodgate, 1st September 1957.

An inspection of the raw materials used in the manufacture of chocolate by Margaret Kunzle, Lord Auchinleck, Dr J.L. Wilson (the Bishop of Birmingham) and Mr G.C. Kunzle (Chairman) at the opening of the new Kunzle factory, Garretts Green Lane, 16th November 1960.

Retirement presentation to Joseph Craig, Norton Motors Ltd., Bracebridge Street, Aston, c. 1962. Mr Craig was the Technical Director in charge of racing motor cycles and his gifts included a mounted Con Rod from a racing Norton.

Midland Red outing to London from Carlyle Works, Edgbaston, 1964.

MIDLAND businessmen had their first 90 m.p.h. luxury lunch on a British train on September 7, 1960.

Dover sole and steak were served as the new blue Pullman express reached its top speed on the Snow Hill to Paddington run.

It was the latest and most impressive development in the diesel train services now operating throughout the Midlands — before the days of electrification.

Mr. George Edwards.

62 years with firm – retires 1964

SEVENTY-NINE - YEAR-OLD Mr. George Edwards, of 26, Glainsdale Road, Hall Green, started work during the Boer War making tools for the assembly of munitions.

Now he has retired after 62 years with Wynn Timmins Ltd., an engineering firm, of Commercial Street.

Mr. Edwards was presented with a cheque by his firm when he reached his 50th year of service, and has now been given a gold watch by his colleagues to mark his retirement.

WHILE THE bulldozers were blasting away at the old New Street Station the chairman of the London Midland Railways Board announced the closure of Snow Hill Station in 1966.

British Rail displayed models of the £4,500,000 development which would give the city a rebuilt New Street.

An initial engineering contract for £2,500,000 was placed with C. Bryant and Son Ltd.

As platforms became rubble — new concrete slabs were being craned into place.

Miraculously the trains still ran. Pedestrians used the old footbridge from Stephenson Place to Station Street to cross the station.

It was the end of a station that opened in 1854 at the then astronomic cost of £500,000.

It was the pride of the steam age — its arched roof the biggest single span in the world.

Award-winning agents meet the management, Britannic Assurance Co. Ltd., Moseley, 21st January 1965.

SEPTEMBER 17 1968

THE FIRST full day of the new two-tier postal system had bankers and businessmen unanimous in their condemnation. The mail just did not get through.

A spokesman for one of the Big Five banks said: "I am plainly worried. We have had only a fraction of our normal correspondence." The new first-class post cost 5d (old pence).

Chairman, T.E. Hurst, opens the doors to the first customers at the new Midland Educational Store (opposite Lewis's), Corporation Street, 8th April 1968. The "Midland Ed", as it was affectionately known, was originally at 41/43 Corporation Street.

1964

BMC — encouraged by the success of the Mini-thinking style which demanded a transverse engine, front wheel drive and wheels at the corners of the car — came out with the Big Car version — the Austin 1800. Prices: saloon £768 (incl. £133 purchase tax); de luxe £808 (£104).

1967

Electricity: Pensioners declared war on the Prime Minister over increased electricity charges. Thousands of elderly people in Birmingham signed a petition to Mr. Wilson asking "Do you want us to freeze this winter?", and a protest march was organised to present it to No. 10 Downing Street.

1969

BIRMINGHAM'S Ann Jones was the newly-crowned Queen of Wimbledon after beating the reigning champion, Billie-Jean King, 3-6, 6-3, 6-2 to win the Ladies' Singles Championship.

After a career spanning 14 years, Mrs. Jones reached the top in her 13th Wimbledon. She received the Gold Plate from Princess Anne and with it went prize money of £1,500.

Hilda Ford, a chargehand cleaner, retires from Miller Street bus depot, 27th September 1968. She and her husband Fred (right) between them worked for Birmingham City Transport for a total of 78 years.

Film star, Barbara Windsor, signs autographs at the Bingley Hall Exhibition, 1970.

BIRMINGHAM telephones go all-number this month.

From April 25 out will go all letter prefixes in the Birmingham telephone area. And in will come ANN—All Numbers Now.

The switch means that there will be no letters-figures duplication for some Birmingham area exchanges.

Exchange names and letters will disappear.

For instance ACOcks Green will no longer exist. At present you can dial ACO or 706 for an Acocks Green number.

But after the changeover it will be 706 only.

The same applies to all other exchanges in the Birmingham area.

From April 25 callers still using letter prefixes will get a pre-recorded announcement referring them to the directory code list.

But after three months the announcement will be scrapped and the number

The new type dial — all figures.

called with a letter prefix will come up as unobtainable.

The switch means that Birmingham will be Britain's first city to switch to all numbers. 1970

The Queen opens the Queensway Ringroad, 7th April 1971.

THE Government has decided that a £10,000,000 national exhibition centre will be built near the Coventry Road at Elmdon. 28/2/70

The retirement of Ruby Price, celebrated by the Sales Accounts Dept., Cadbury's, 1st October 1971.

The staff of Eddystone Radio Ltd., gather to celebrate the company's 50th anniversary, Alvechurch Road, West Heath, 1st August 1973.

Despite being blind for twenty years Michael Townsend, of Selly Oak, has obtained his master's degree in computer science. His guide dog, Beatle, was named after the group which financed its training. 17th December 1976.

It's a hands-on approach for the charity netball team of David F. Wiseman & Sons Ltd. (plumbers), Moseley Road, 1973.

Steve Race, of "My Music" fame, draws the winner of the GKN "Music to your Ears" competition at the International Spring Fair held at the NEC, 1979.

Jean Vaughan meets the Duke of Kent, Burman & Sons Ltd (mfrs. of steering gears, etc.), Wychall Lane, Kings Norton, 1977.

The Birmingham Post, Monday, February 2, 1976

SPECIAL MESSAGE FROM THE PRIME MINISTER

For the first time Britain has an exhibition complex at least equal to anything to be found elsewhere in Europe.

The fact that we can at last show our goods in a truly worthy setting will be a major asset in our efforts to increase our share of world exports.

So the contribution which the new National Exhibition Centre can make to the future prosperity of Birmingham, the region and Britain is enormous.

Having supported the proposal back in 1970, I am delighted that it has now come to fruition. I offer my congratulations to the City Council, the Company, the Chamber of Commerce and everyone who has had a hand in seeing this massive project through.

Harold Wilson

35

George Rawlins (group chairman) of Rawlins Bros. Ltd., Drews Lane, Washwood Heath, practises for the Centenary Procession in Sutton Coldfield, April 1979.

Simon Yates toasts the succcess of Davenports' continental lager after it had won the 20th Monde Selection competition in Amsterdam. Bath Row, 7th August 1981.

Lady Hobday cuts the cake as she welcomes Central Independent Television to Birmingham, on the first day of broadcasting, 1st January 1982. The Master of Ceremonies, at the microphone, is Shaw Taylor.

Welcome to
Lloyds British National Golf Day
at the Belfry Hotel, Lichfield Road,
Wishaw, Sutton Coldfield,

on

Friday, 26 September 1986.

Central Independent Television news presenters (from left) Anne Dawson and Wesley Smith (Central South), Anna Soubry (Central East), Bob Warman (Central West), Anne Davies (Central East), Bob Hall and Michele Newman (Central West), 1984.

With a cheer from his workmates postman/driver, Doug Marshall, brings his last collection into Severn Street Post Office, 12th December 1986. He had just completed 50 years service.

As part of a traditional retirement ceremony bus driver, Robert Ward, is towed into Washwood Heath depot by some of his workmates, 28th February 1989.

Alton, engaged as Guest Speaker at the AGM of the Midland Association of Restaurants Caterers and Hotels, stands (centre) with, from left to right, Paul Clayton-Smith (Midland Hotel), Judith Foster (Association Secretary) Stephen Carter (Holiday Inn) and Graham Golby (Metropole Hotel and Conference Centre), Holiday Inn, 22nd March 1988.

BRMB Radio Personality, Les Ross (left), and model, Maria Whittaker, with Marketing Director, John Cavey, launch a telephone information service to help pub-goers make the most of their leisure-time, Brasshouse on Broad Street, 9th November 1989.

The International Conference Centre is declared officially open by the Queen, 12th June 1991.

The children help Lyn Jones to celebrate his 50th birthday, whilst his wife Christine looks on, Mickleton Nurseries, Norman Road, Northfield, 21st April 1993. Chris and Lyn are the proprietors of three pre-school nurseries in Northfield.

REFRESHMENT BREAK

Star Vaults, Dale End, 17th February 1955.

Red Cow, Horse Fair, 4th December 1956.

Hobson Road/Pershore Road, Selly Park, 9th November 1954.

Royal Exchange, High Street/Alma Street, Aston, 15th November 1956.

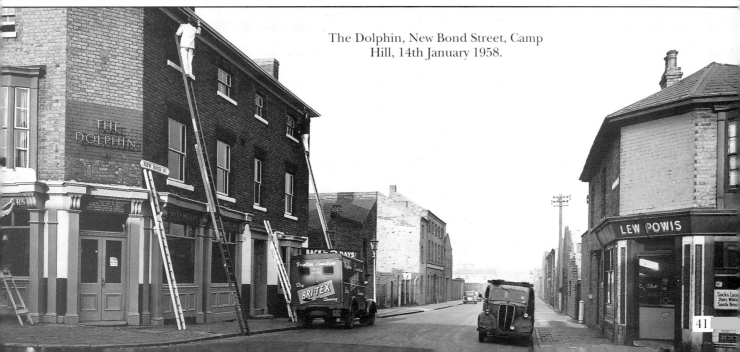

The Dolphin, New Bond Street, Camp Hill, 14th January 1958.

Swan With Two Necks, Lawley Street/Great Brook Street, 11th February 1959.

Gladstone Place, Asylum Road, Newtown, 23rd May 1960.

Josie's Cafe, Prince Albert Street/Green Lane, Small Heath, 22nd March 1961.

Joyce's Cafe, Taunton Road/Roshven Road, Sparkbrook, 19th September 1962.

Custard House, Blake Lane, Bordesley Green, 1962.

Cateswell Cafe, Stratford Road, Hall Green, 1962.

Lime Tree Road, Washwood Heath, February 1967.

The Fox, Hurst Street, just across from the Hippodrome, 21st February 1967.

The Bartons Arms, High Street, Aston, 31st May 1967.

The Warstone, Icknield Street/Camden Street, 14th August 1967.

Stan's Cafe, Headingley Road, Handsworth, 10th July 1967.

Farm Street/Bridge Street West,
Hockley, 27th February 1968.

"THAT REMINDS ME—
WE MUST GO TO THE "EXCHANGE" GRILL
AFTERWARDS— THE FOOD THERE
IS ABSOLUTELY
FIRST-CLASS"

"EXCHANGE"
GRILL & RESTAURANT
JUST ROUND THE CORNER IN STEPHENSON PLACE

TEAS +++ DINNERS +++ SUPPERS

PROPRIETORS:
Mitchells & Butlers

"Good Fare & Good Honest Beer"

Michael's Cafe, Station Road/Witton Lane, Aston,
14th August 1968.

PICKWICK COFFEE HOUSE
8 NEEDLESS ALLEY
BIRMINGHAM

Shaftmoor Lane, Hall Green, 5th November 1969.

Railway Terrace/Nechells Park Road, 26th February 1973.

Union Street/High Street, 13th July 1973.

The workforce, from William Sapcote & Sons, employed to build Jenkins Street bridge, Small Heath, c. 1905. Incidentally, the firm celebrated 140 years of business in 1993.

Birmingham University Council and Academy and Staff, 1901. Joseph Chamberlain, who was Chancellor, sits in the centre of the front row.

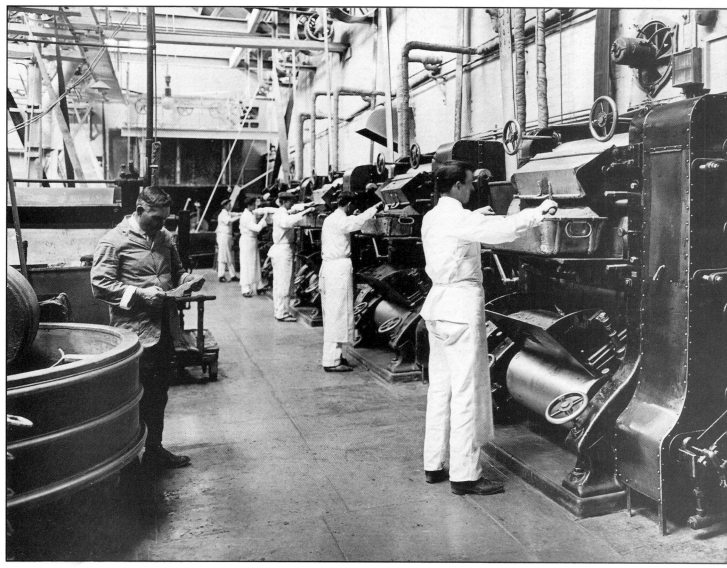

Cadbury employees working on a mixer and a battery of chocolate
rolls to grind cocoa and sugar, 1912.

Austin Motor Co. Ltd., Longbridge, c. 1912.

The Birmingham Daily Mail

WEDNESDAY, AUGUST 5, 1914.

SE5a Aircraft, South Works, Austin Motor Co. Ltd., Longbridge, 1917.

Kalamazoo (sales) Ltd. (loose leaf books and office systems), Mill Lane, Northfield, c. 1920.

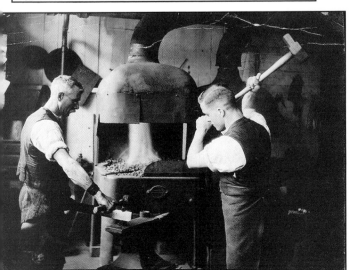

Blacksmiths at work at Compton & Hickman, Bristol Road, Selly Oak, c. 1920

Chocolate decorating, Cadbury's, 1922.

Fitting Shop, Austin Motor Co. Ltd., Longbridge, c. 1923. The foreman
(in white coat on left) is Harry Church.

Harry Mason on his greengrocery round, Stirchley, 1924.

Turner Bros., River Street/Longmore Street, Balsall Heath, c. 1925.

Mrs Webster views potential customers, Factory Road,
Soho, 3rd March 1927.

Cottage loaves being put into the ovens, George Baines Ltd., Finch Road, Handsworth, c. 1925.

THERE are 2,000,000 unemployed as summer begins to fade. 1930

A man called Hitler has his picture in the "Mail" for the first time. Unrest threatens in India, the Labour Government is on its last legs.

But if you are not on the dole, Birmingham is a great place for a night out.

In the first week of September the pre-London production of a new play, "The Barretts of Wimpole Street," is at the Repertory Theatre with Cedrick Hardwicke and Gwen Ffrangcon-Davies.

The Theatre Royal has a pre-London visit from Gertrude Lawrence, Noel Coward and Laurence Olivier in a comedy called "Private Lives."

Albert Sandler and Jimmy James are at the Hippodrome; Flanagan and Allen at the Aston Hippodrome. The Futurist is showing Gary Cooper in "The Virginian" . . .

Enter Sophie...

In the next week a "raucous" American called Sophie Tucker appears in a new musical show at the Royal with Jack and Claude Hulbert. This will soon be replaced by the pre-London showing of "It's a Boy," with Leslie Henson and Sydney Howard.

And the Hippodrome is about to welcome a new overseas act. The "Mail" critic writes: "From America come Mr. George Burns and Miss Grace Allen, a patter and song duo by whom a whimsical note is struck . . ."

McNamara road transporters loaded up with crated motor cycles from Norton Motors Ltd., Aston Brook Street, c. 1930.

BIRMINGHAM STOCK EXCHANGE.

MARKETS GENERALLY QUIET AND DEPRESSED.

BIRMINGHAM, Friday.—There was no improvement in business, and the markets wore a depressed appearance, the development in Shanghai having an adverse effect. British Government securities were much quieter, and both conversion and War Loans slowly declined. Corporation stocks were featureless, and a moderate business in Bank shares had little effect upon prices, Lloyds finishing a trifle lower at 45s. 3d. Among Insurance issues, Royals were easier at 6¾.

The leading Industrials were marked down in conformity with the general tendency, so that the advances established in the early part of the week practically disappeared. Courtaulds were more plentiful, and steadily declined to 33s. 6d. on renewed dividend discussion. J. and P. Coats were steady at 39s. 9d., but Tobacco shares weakened, Imperials giving way to 80s. 3d., and British-Americans to 78s. 9d. Anglo-American shares were generally lower, International Nickels being down to 11½, and Electric and Musicals to 20s. Woolworths were quieter and reacted to 49s. 9d., but Marks and Spencers remained firm.

Imperial Chemicals were quiet, and both Ordinary and Deferred lost ground. Turner and Newalls continued to react, and Pinchin Johnsons and Dunlop Rubbers also were easier.

CYCLE, MOTOR AND TYRE SHARES.

30.1.32

MODERATE DEALINGS.

BIRMINGHAM, Friday.—A modest business in Motor shares had little effect on prices. Austin Ordinary lost part of their recent advance, changing hands at the lower figure of 25s., while the "B" Preference were steady at 16s. 6d. Rovers were still in favour, being dealt in at the higher figure of 3s., New Hudsons improved a little, Rolls-Royce were still strong, and Standards were again fairly active, with a further advance to 25s. 6d. Fords weakened again, but Guys and Leylands were both the turn better, and Singers were still hard.

RISE: Standard Motors, 3d.

FALLS: Austin Motor Ord., 9d.; Ford Motor, 6d.

TRANSACTIONS.

Austin, 25,0	Rover (8,0), 3/0
B Pref., 16/6	Standard, 25,6 §25/4½
Guy, 2,11¼	§25,7½

CLOSING PRICES.

	Buyers.	Sellers.		Buyers.	Sellers.
Austin A Pf.		19,6	Leyland	32,0	32,9
Pfd.	11/6		Mulliners		0,3
Db.		96¾	New Hudson	2,7½	
Bluemel Bros.	15,0	17,6	Riley (Cov.)		31/0
Pf.		18,0	Rolls-Royce	30,0	
Components	1,6		S.T.D. Motors	0,7½	
Dfd.	1,6		Pfd. Ord.	2,0	
Pf	8,0		Serck Rad.		31/0
Dennis Bros.	18,3	18,9	Singer		7/3
Fodens		8,6	Pf.		10,0
Ford	32,9	33/11½	Standard		25,6
Guy	2,6	3,3	Triumph		7,6
Halford	43,0	45/0	Pf.		15,9
Hermetic Rbr.	15,0				

§For new account.

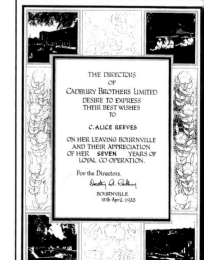

Bottling at H P Sauce Ltd., Aston, 9th September 1935.

Motor cycles being checked over, prior to dispatch,
Norton Motors Ltd., sometime in the thirties.

Alum Rock Road/Gowan Road, Alum Rock, 1935.

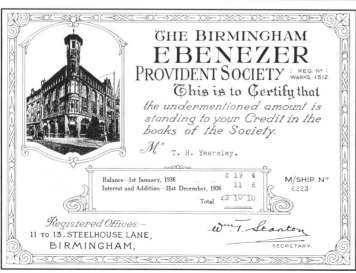

Birmingham Police, "E" Division,
Hay Mills Police Station, c. 1939.

"German propaganda makes the most of the attacks on British factories. This must have a heartening effect on German morale. We, on the other hand, do not permit the slightest verbosity on our accounts of bombing Germany. A little verbosity here and there might be rather encouraging."
— *Home Intelligence Report to the Ministry of Information.*

1940

1940

On the nights of the raids Cadbury's sent two vans around the city dispensing cocoa to bombed out victims and rescue workers.

The returning van drivers told the night shift workers where bombs had fallen. Many men left their benches and went in search of their families.

Other than losing pay for time lost these absentees were not penalised.

— *Ministry of the Home Security report on Cadbury's*

26.4.40

HOW PRICES of drinks and tobacco have increased owing to the Budget can be seen from the following table: Draught beer 5d increased to 6d a pint, ale 7d to 8d a pint, tobacco 11d to 1s 2d an ounce, cigarettes (10) 5d to 6d, cigarettes (10) 7d to 8½.

Birmingham Mail

18.8.40

LEMONS are unobtainable in Birmingham. This is by no means surprising since Italy and Spain are the source of the supply.

"I haven't a lemon in the shop," confessed a fruiterer today, "and I don't give much for your chance of getting any. There may be a few during the next day or two, when a ship comes in, but the scarcity is certain to continue."

English apples may be had in a wide range, with Worcester Pearmains popular at 8d. to 10d. per lb. Imported apples are costing 10d. per lb. and cookers 3d. to 4d. Cultivated blackberries are available at 1s. per lb. Oranges are from 2s. to 3s. per dozen, according to size, and grapefruit 6d. each.

Buying Office, Austin Motor Co. Ltd., Longbridge, 1942.

Jerry Can production, Austin Motor Co. Ltd., Longbridge, c. 1943.

Transporting a Sterling fuselage from East Works, Austin Aeroplane Factory, Longbridge, c. 1942.

Castle Bromwich Aeroplane Factory F.C., 1942.

Officers and N.C.O's of the 52nd Battalion Home Guard,
Castle Bromwich Aeroplane Factory, 1943.

SIR,—I should like to register an emphatic protest against the threatened "cut" in the meat ration. I do this, not because it is unnecessary, but because the Ministry of Food is treating the matter in the wrong way.

It is well known that a great number of people, because of high wages or because they have other means, augment their meat ration by dining at works canteens, British Restaurants or the higher-priced cafes, etc., which means that if you have sufficient money you can have the whole of your meat ration at the week-end, while thousands of the poorer-paid people have to live on their bare rations.

This is very unfair and makes a mockery of the rationing scheme.

I suggest, therefore, that instead of cutting the meat ration, the Ministry of Food increases it by at least 4d. per head, and issues a card to every person, to be date-stamped when purchasing a meat course at a restaurant or canteen and 2d. taken off the meat ration when purchasing meat from a butcher's shop.

Besides this, rabbits, poultry, game and offal could be included in the ration.

16.5.45   F. W. PRICE.

BACK AT WORK AGAIN 11/5/45

After two days and nights of whole-hearted rejoicing Birmingham workpeople went back yesterday with a unanimity that surprised many personnel managers who had been anticipating a "morning after" attendance.

In many of the large works throughout the city the report was the same—practically 100 per cent. attendance, except for a few laggards.

Blue Watch, "F" Division, Ward End, National Fire Service, 1945.

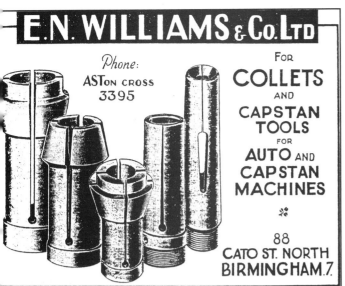
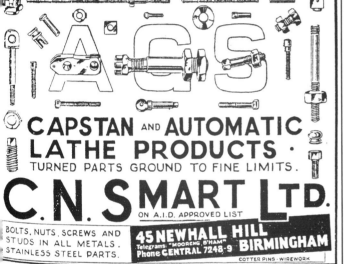

Addison Road, Kings Heath, 1947.

Due to the terrible weather, in 1947, the GEC works at Witton were closed down until things improved.
Then, telegrams were sent out, recalling the workers. Here, we see toolmakers on their first day back.

Court Road, Balsall Heath, 23rd August 1949.

Bristol Street, 7th September 1949.

Testing of electrical control panels at Donovan Electrical Co. Ltd., Northcote Road, Stechford, 1950.

Frankley Beeches Road, Northfield, 4th January 1950.

King's Road, Tyseley, 5th October 1950.

Bristol Road, Northfield, 12th July 1950.

Coleshill Street, 5th October 1950.

Slade Road, Erdington, 26th January 1951.

Aston Hall Road, 31st May 1951.

Holdings Garage, Raddlebarn Road,
Selly Oak, 22nd November 1951.

After eighty years of service the steamroller-type shunting engine, John Barleycorn, is about to retire from active service, Mitchells & Butlers, Cape Hill, December 1951.

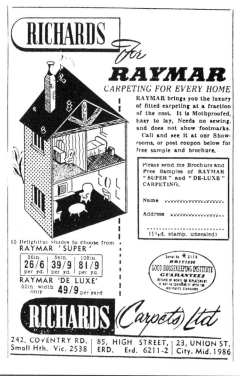

Booths Farm Road, Perry Barr, c. 1952.

Old Mews Garage, Redditch Road, Kings Norton, 8th February 1952.

Digbeth, 26th June 1952.

Dunlop Rubber Co. Ltd., Fort Dunlop, Erdington, 27th November 1952.

Melvina Road, Vauxhall, 12th December 1952.

High Street, Kings Heath, 17th June 1953.

Great Lister Street, Nechells, 12th December 1952.

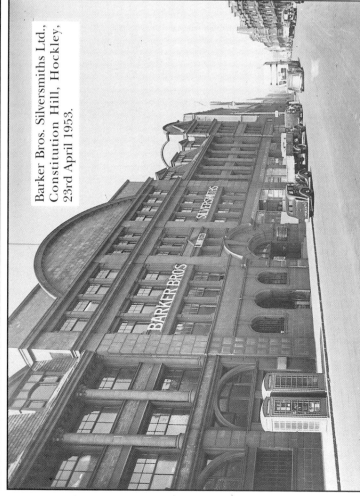

Barker Bros. Silversmiths Ltd., Constitution Hill, Hockley, 23rd April 1953.

Vicarage Road, Kings Heath, July 1953.

Sure shield against chills

Portable warmth—when you want it and where you want it! Millions already in use. Ask to see the new models.

Valor HEATERS

The sign of the genuine Valor.

Manufactured by THE VALOR CO. LTD. (Regd. Proprietors) BIRMINGHAM.

VALOR REPAIR SERVICE

The manufacturers of Valor maintain an incomparable service of repair parts. There's no shortage of Valor repair parts.

Wholesale Distributors in U.K.
ANGLO-AMERICAN OIL COMPANY LTD.

ALWAYS USE ESSO ROYAL DAYLIGHT PARAFFIN
C.H.I.

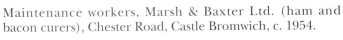

Maintenance workers, Marsh & Baxter Ltd. (ham and bacon curers), Chester Road, Castle Bromwich, c. 1954.

High Street, Bordesley, 3rd September 1953.

Pinnick's Radio & Television Co. Ltd., Alcester Road South, Kings Heath, 1954.

A reflective pause for José Austin (nee Moss), Ministry of Pensions & National Insurance, Kingstanding Road, Kingstanding, c. 1955.

Joseph Lucas Ltd. (automobile electrical equipment), Great Hampton Street/Hockley Street, 25th October 1954.

Eric Reeves goes to work with an oxy-acetylene cutter, Birmingham Co-operative Society Ltd. Garages, Great Brook Street, Vauxhall, c. 1955.

Payton, Pepper & Sons Ltd. (mfng jewellers), Vyse Street, Hockley, c. 1955.

What a lot of jobs!

THERE was no shortage of jobs in 1955. It went on record as the year 50,000 vacancies were chasing workers in the Midlands.

It was an era of virtual full-employment, when the number of people in work was the highest on record.

The peak figure for outstanding jobs was recorded in July — 57,883. According to official reports this figure fell "quite sharply" in November — down to 50,000.

The highest peak of unemployment was in January when 11,428 were out of work, but this was 5,000 fewer than 1954. The lowest unemployment count was in July when the figure was 8,564.

The percentage of unemployed among a working population of more than two million in the West Midlands was never more than 0.5 per cent.

Stratford Road, Sparkbrook, 27th January 1955.

Station Road, Harborne, 6th June 1955.

Thornley & Knight Ltd. (paint, varnish, enamel and lacquer mfrs), Bordesley Green Road, 23rd February 1956.

High Street/Ravenhurst Road, Harborne, 21st November 1955.

Watery Lane, Bordesley, 8th May 1956.

Birmingham Co-operative Society Ltd. Workshops,
Ashted Row, Nechells Green, 28th August 1956.

Digbeth, with Meriden Street on the right,
11th September 1956.

Vittoria Street, Hockley, 5th June 1956.

High Street, Aston, 4th January 1957.

Bristol Road, Selly Oak, 29th January 1957.

District Nurses off on their rounds, Summer Hill Road,
Spring Hill, 30th May 1957.

A.J. Gilbert (B'ham) Ltd. (press workers etc.),
Buckingham Street, Hockley, 18th July 1957.

Chester Road, Erdington, 28th January 1958.

Warwick Road, Acocks Green, 7th October 1957.

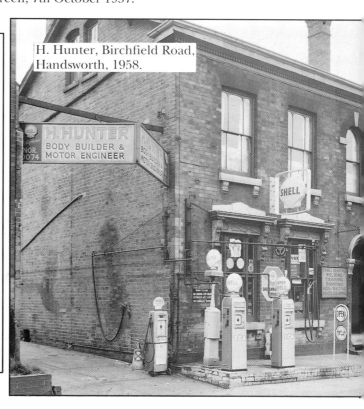

H. Hunter, Birchfield Road, Handsworth, 1958.

British Timken Ltd. (mfrs of bar and roller bearings), Cheston Road, Aston, 28th March 1958.

Toolmaking at H.E. Hazlehurst Ltd., Darwin Street, Highgate, 5th December 1958.

Stratford Road, Sparkbrook, 5th June 1959.

The construction of Lea Mason School, Lee Bank Road, Edgbaston, 31st July 1959.

Tree-removing, Bell Barn Road, Lee Bank, 1958.

Monument Road/Wood Street, Ladywood, 13th August 1959.

Super Oil Seals & Gaskets Ltd., Factory Centre, Kings Norton, 11th March 1960.

Export Office staff, Cadbury Bros. Ltd., Bournville, 1960.

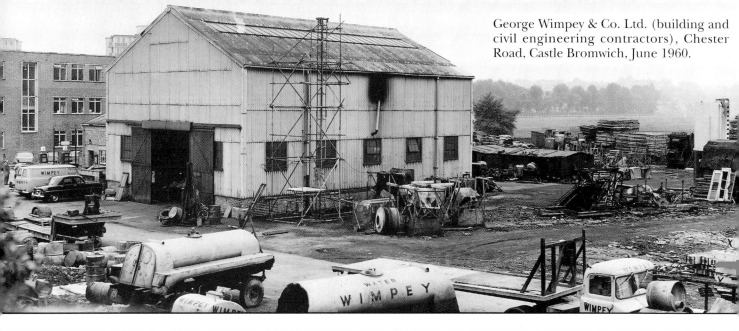

George Wimpey & Co. Ltd. (building and civil engineering contractors), Chester Road, Castle Bromwich, June 1960.

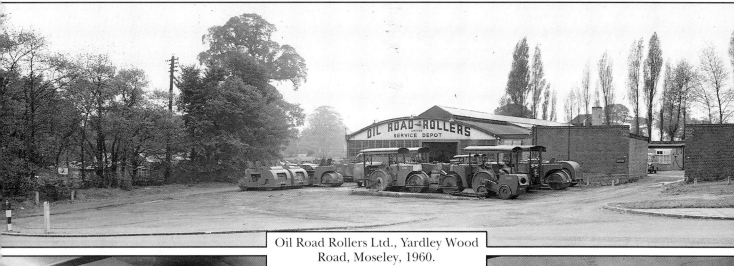

Oil Road Rollers Ltd., Yardley Wood Road, Moseley, 1960.

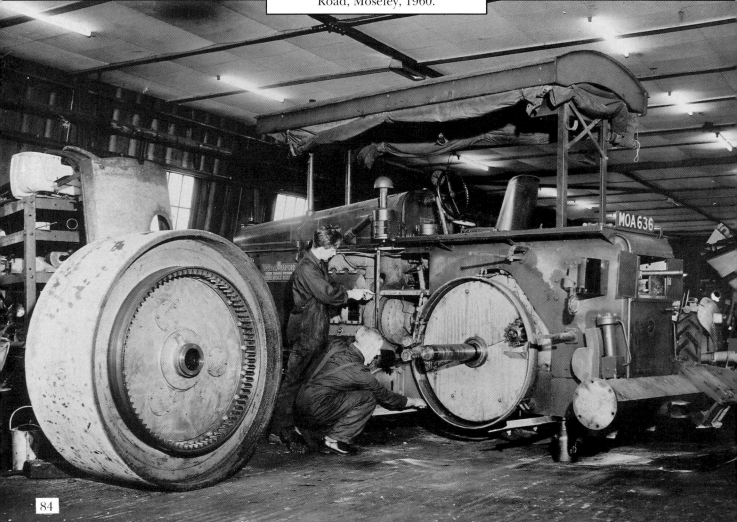

Warwick Road, Acocks Green, 15th August 1960.

Hughes Lathbury Ltd. (press workers), Hospital Street/New Summer Street, Newtown, 21st June 1960.

Craelius Co. Ltd. (diamond core and concrete drilling mfrs), Rock Spring Works, Cheston Road, Aston, c. 1960.

United Artists Picture Corporation (film hirers), Lee Bank House, Holloway Head, 7th March 1961.

Midland Stationers Ltd., Lee Bank House, Holloway Head, 1961.

Val Fisher, (now Val Hastings) typist-sales promotions, Bristol Street Motors, Sherlock Street, 1961. Incidentally, she now runs a highly successful agency for actors.

The Walpamur Co. Ltd. (paints), George Street West, Spring Hill, 1961.

Deutsch & Brenner Ltd. (non-ferrous metal mfrs), Barr Street/Harford Street, Hockley, 26th January 1961.

Calthorpe Road, Edgbaston, 15th March 1961.

Diecastings Ltd., Highgate Square, Highgate, 8th September 1961.

Leonard Woolley Ltd. (metal shearers), Leopold Street, Highgate,
23rd October 1961.

Birmingham Waste Co. Ltd., Moland Mills, Belmont Row, Nechells Green, 17th October 1961.

Station Road/Northcote Road, Stechford, 7th November 1961.

Birmingham Municipal Bank, Bordesley Green, 16th January 1962.

Marsh Lane, Stockland Green, 11th February 1963.

Commercial Street, 14th June 1962.

Tesco, Coventry Road, Small Heath, November 1963.

R. White's (soft drinks), Western Road, Spring Hill, 1963.

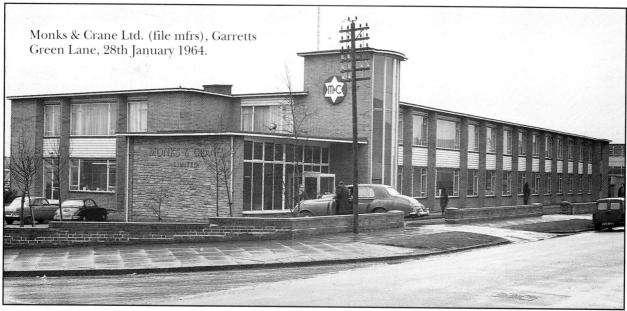

Monks & Crane Ltd. (file mfrs), Garretts Green Lane, 28th January 1964.

Bromsgrove Street, 14th February 1964.

Aston Road North, Aston, 18th December 1963.

William H. Painter Ltd. (funeral directors),
Yardley Road, South Yardley, 1965.

Teaching Staff, Yenton Junior School, Chester Road, Erdington, 1965.

Westley Road, Acocks Green, 6th April 1965.

Victor E. Turton (Tools) Ltd. (engineers merchants, small tools, factory equipment), Plume Street, Aston, 15th September 1965.

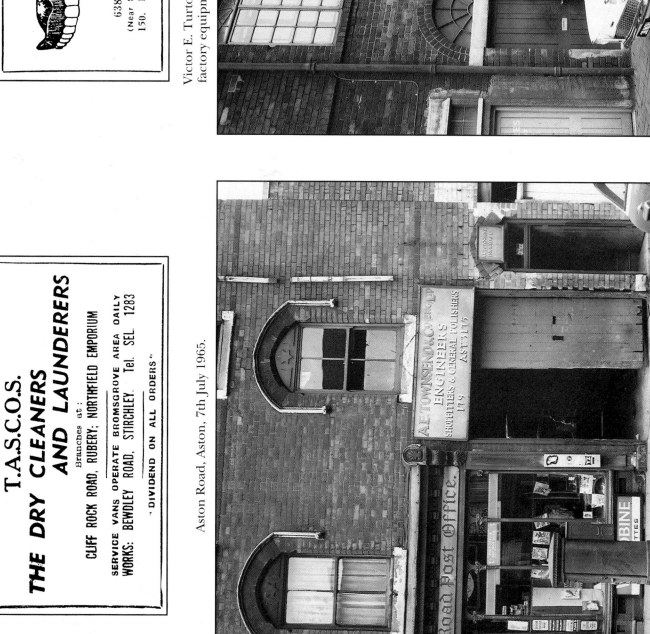

Aston Road, Aston, 7th July 1965.

Park Garage Autos (B'ham) Ltd., Warwards Lane, Selly Oak, 31st May 1965.

Bromford Lane, 12th October 1965.

Villa Road, Handsworth, 29th April 1966.

Washwood Heath Road, Ward End, 17th December 1965.

Mary Dorrell sorts out the stock in her pawnbroker's shop, Leopold Street, Balsall Heath, 8th November 1966.

Smith's Potato Crisps, Wharfd
Road, Acocks Green, 1966.

Christine Barlow using a stitching machine,
Boxfoldia Ltd., Dale Road, Bournbrook, 1967.

Alcester Road, Moseley, 1967.

Instead of spending Christmas on his honeymoon, Yenton footballer, Fred Sinnot, finds himself in hospital recovering from rheumatic fever. Keeping his spirits up are student nurses, Jean Musgrove and Elaine Smith and Staff Nurse Judy Arter, Birmingham General Hospital, Steelhouse Lane, 1967.

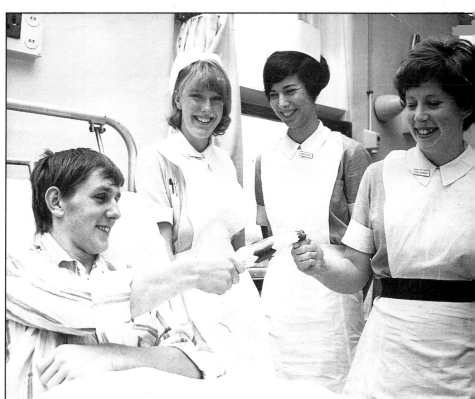

Typing Pool, Patrick Motors, Bristol Road, Selly Oak, c. 1967.

Spring Hill, with Ellen Street on the right, 17th August 1967.

R.G. Kemp (motor accessories), Redditch Road/The Green, Kings Norton, 11th October 1967.

Chad Valley Works (toy mfrs), Rose Road, Harborne, 19th October 1967.

Sankeys (central heating, etc.), Bartholomew Street/Banbury Street, 26th October 1967.

The City has always been renowned for the quality of its jewellery. This quartet of photographs were all taken in the Jewellery Quarter, in Hockley, in 1967.

W.H. Tandy & Sons (fancy ring makers), Vyse Street.

E. & S. Brown Ltd. (mfng. jewellers), Vyse Street.

Making metal moulds at Gladman and Norman Ltd. (badge mfrs). Spencer Street.

Eaton & Wrighton Ltd. (gold ring makers), Vyse Street.

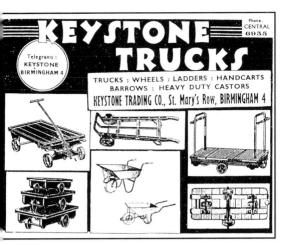

Electrical Dept., Midland Red Central Works, Carlyle Road, Edgbaston, 1968.

Warwick Road, Tyseley, February 1968.

Andy's Coaches, Nechells Park Road, Nechells, 11th March 1968.

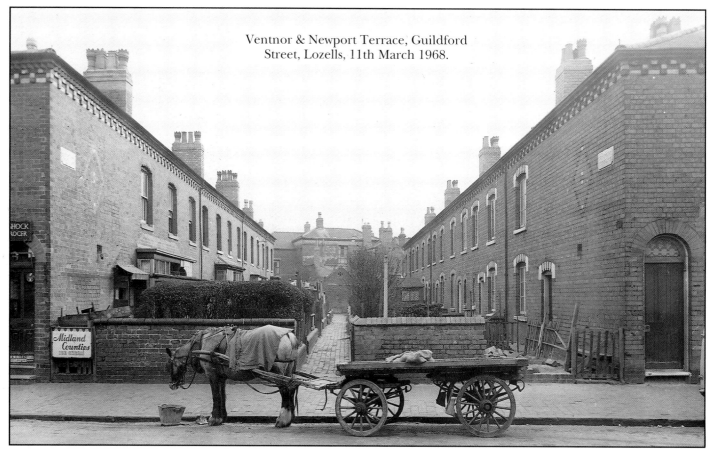

Ventnor & Newport Terrace, Guildford Street, Lozells, 11th March 1968.

Gravelley Hill Motorway under construction, 5th March 1969.

Firemen endeavour to stop the flow of water from a burst main in Spring Hill, 5th August 1968.

R. Twining & Co. Ltd. (tea and coffee merchants),
Ladywell Walk, Highgate, 17th May 1968.

Slumberland Ltd. (bedding mfrs),
Redfern Road, Acocks Green,
25th July 1968.

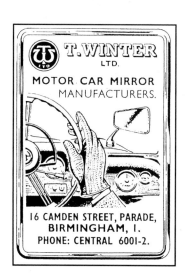
Arthur R. Price (Aston Manor)
Ltd. (motor accessories), Park
Lane, Aston, 1968.

Birchfield Caravans, Heathfield Road, Handsworth, November 1968.

Ansells Brewery, Lichfield Road, Aston, 26th October 1969.

Thomas Haddon & Stokes Ltd. (mfrs of metal thread
screws, etc.), High Street, Deritend, 29th October 1969.

Coventry Road/Camp Hill, 10th February 1970.

Birmingham Airport, 28th April 1970.

11.2.70.

The 3½-mile Quinton to Oldbury section of the £18 million M5-M6 link should be open next month, the Ministry of Transport forecast yesterday.

The remaining sections between Oldbury and Bescot, are scheduled to open in May.

Finishing work is now being done on the first stretch, which will bring traffic into the heart of the Black Country.

Morris Commercial Cars Ltd., West Plant, Bordesley Green Road, Adderley Park, 4th December 1970.

Patrick Motors Ltd., Longbridge Lane, 18th October 1971.

Rubery Quarry, Cock Hill Lane, Rubery, 15th November 1971.

Preparing for 'D-Day'

1970

BIRMINGHAM'S 14,000 small shopkeepers are being asked to "go back to school" to learn the rudiments of decimalisation.

The scheme, which is being sponsored by the National Chamber of Trade and Birmingham Education Committee, urges shopkeepers to attend a special course at Lea Mason Adult Adult Education Centre, Birmingham, starting on January 4.

Mr. T. N. Hains, West Midland area secretary of the Chamber of Trade, said the idea was to prepare shopkeepers fully for when decimalisation comes into force in February 1971.

"Large stores have their own training schemes and that is why we are concentrating on the small shopkeepers," he said. "The idea is to see how well they can cope with the new money."

The scheme, which is being run all over the country, is being subsidised by the Distributive Industries Training Board.

Bingo hall plea

An application for planning permission for a Bingo hall at Chelmsley Wood shopping centre has been made to Meriden Rural District Council by Bryant-Samuel Ltd.

Brewery Street, Handsworth, 18th February 1972.

House building begins, Coombes Lane, Northfield, 23rd November 1971.

1971

MAY I comment on the article, "The Meat That Isn't" — imitation meat.

The people who are to judge are the customers.

Have people noticed the almost complete absence of English beef in supermarkets over the past few weeks?

In my opinion the markets dictate what managers want you to eat.

In the coming week it will no doubt be poultry, the frozen kind,

Incidentally, why have the markets not thought of a separate entrance so that one could pop in and buy a couple of chops or a steak without the irksome task of going through the same ritual as the person who is purchasing her week's entire shopping?

Full marks to the campaign against the introduction of soya bean meat.

T-Bone Lover.
Yardley.

Warwards Lane/Milner Road, Stirchley, 1st January 1973.

Chester Road, Castle Bromwich, 24th September 1974.

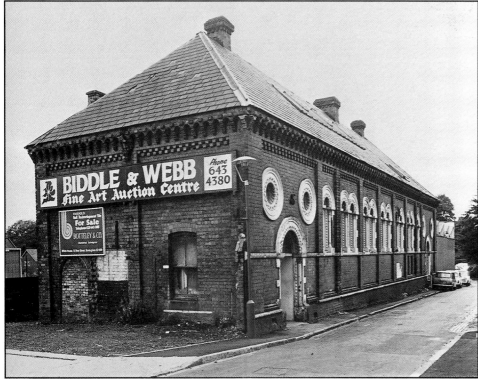

Enfield Hall, Enfield Road/Islington Row, 1974.

Aldridge Road/Queslett Road, Great Barr, 16th October 1972.

Stratford Road, Hall Green, 11th October 1974.

A public meeting at the Sutton Coldfield Town Hall, 20th June 1975.

114

Bordesley Street/New Canal Street, 4th May 1976.

F. & J. Black Ltd. (builders), Berkeley Road, Hay Mills, 15th June 1976.

Bablin Hairdressing Salon, immediately after refurbishment, Bristol Road South, Northfield, 14th March 1984.

Tom Stirk, Peter Wallace and Eric Mortiboy proudly show off
their new dustmen's outfits, 7th April 1984.

Ivy and Ron Tennant are about to retire from shop-keeping in Warwick Road, Tyseley, 18th November 1984. Ron's family had owned the shop for over half a century.

Smaller shopkeepers are disappearing, with a third of Birmingham's shops having vanished in 30 years, says a report to city planners.

But old-style local High Street centres will still be the firm favourite for shoppers for the next ten years, it adds.

The report on shopping trends was prepared by city officials to help the planners to work out a policy on how shopping arrangements in the city should develop.

The report, which went before a recent planning committee meeting, said there were nearly 20,000 retail outlets, including corner shops, in Birmingham in 1950. Now there were only 12,500.

But the officials said that this did not mean there were less shopping facilities, because new traders who had opened up since, tended to have bigger premises.

The report added that planners had been under pressure to allow more big bulk-buying supermarkets on the edge of the city for car-borne shoppers, in recent years.

But it added that High Street type centres would continue being the favourite of most shoppers for the rest of the decade because of travel costs.

The committee agreed to think about giving more support to projects to revitalise declining older shopping centres in future.

A familiar sight in Kings Norton and Cotteridge, Peter Buckley sets out to sweep the streets clean, Pershore Road South, 17th September 1986.

Philip Hemingway, with employees Kathleen Doran, Linda Quinney and John Dale, prepare for Christmas, Newtown Shopping Centre, December 1988.

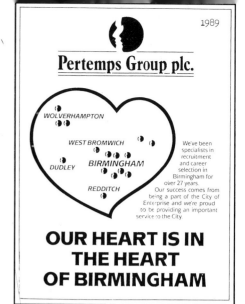

Parade, Sutton Coldfield, 14th March 1988.

Workers dig away the snow to free an articulated vehicle
in Island Road, Handsworth, 8th December 1990.

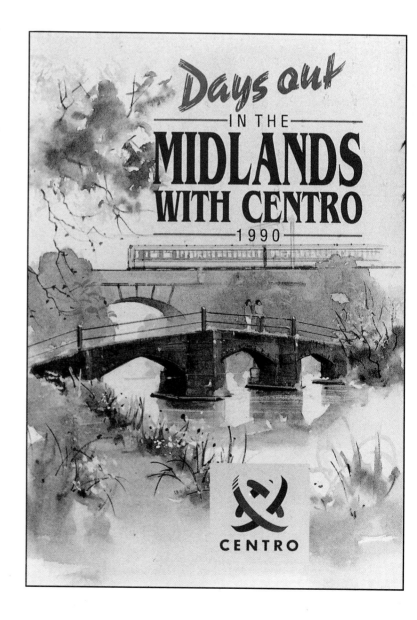

L E W I S'S

Situated on the corner of Bull Street and Corporation Street, backing on to The Old Square, Lewis's opened in 1885 and finally closed its doors on 13th July 1991. In those intervening years it was held in great affection by Brummies. Here, we show just a tiny sample of items as our tribute to possibly one of the last large stores ever to grace the City.

LEWIS'S SALE
REMNANT
and
ODDMENT DAY
1925
to-morrow!

For the FIRST TIME during the SALE

THOUSANDS of REMNANTS

SILKS, ARTIFICIAL SILKS,
DRESS FABRICS, COTTON FABRICS,
VELVETEENS, LININGS, DRAPERY,
ON THE

FOURTH FLOOR
in LEWIS'S Store

The marked prices for these afford a most wonderful opportunity for saving. FRIDAY is the only REMNANT DAY and the record Bargain prices will remain unchanged till all are cleared.
In addition there are Thousands of ODDMENTS on every floor in BOTH BUILDINGS TO-MORROW

COME AT NINE!

Lewis's Sale ends on Saturday

Jan Berenska and his orchestra playing in the Ranelagh Room restaurant, c. 1937.

Looking down Corporation Street, towards the Central Fire Station, with Lewis's on the left, 1960.

Employees in the Roof Garden, 1957.

Margaret and Hazel Scott in Pet's Corner, 1964.

Recording stars, the Kaye Sisters, cut into a cake-replica of the Birmingham store, 16th April 1967. The occasion was to commemorate the 111th anniversary of the opening of the first Lewis's store in Liverpool. Otto Wuest created the 56lb cake and an exact cardboard replica appeared in the window in Corporation Street.

city centre
SPRING FESTIVAL
May 18·30th 1970

LEWIS'S

L EWIS'S have entered into the spirit of this important event in the life of our great city by providing a host of exciting attractions, competitions, special displays and demonstrations with the co-operation of many well-known manufacturers.

There is something to interest every member of the family—young and old alike—and we take this opportunity (reflected in the little badges worn by our staff for this special fortnight) of saying "Welcome to Lewis's."

ATTRACTIONS

A FORMAL FLOWER GARDEN planted with trees, plants, and featuring lovely garden pools (Minories).

THE WORLD'S LARGEST WORKING MODEL INTERNATIONAL AIRPORT with 100 planes and 1,000 vehicles. Capt. Carney will operate it hourly throughout the day (5th Floor).

FASHION PARADES COMPERED BY OLGA YATES the famous London Fashion Consultant.

18th-22nd May. Parades of Holiday Fashions showing the easy way to travel — at 12 noon, 1 p.m., 2 p.m. and 4 p.m. (Ground Floor).

25th-29th May. Formal Fashion Parades—at 11.30 a.m., 1 p.m. and 3 p.m. (additional parade on Thursday, 5 p.m.). (Second Floor).

MISS JANE GILKS (by courtesy of L'Oreal of Paris) a member of England's World Cup Hairstyling Team will demonstrate her new 'Festival' Hairstyle, specially created for this event. May 26th-28th May. (Second Floor).

STROMBOLI THE SWORD SWALLOWER will appear at the Wilkinson Sword counter 26h-28h. (Second Floor).

MR. BARRY TWOMLOW, News of the World Darts Champion, will demonstrate his skill with Unicorn Darts on Saturday, May 23rd. (Fifth Floor).

CHILDREN'S PLAY AREA, with swings, etc. Try out the 'Spacehoppers', see demonstrations of toys by many leading makers. (Fifth Floor).

COMPETITIONS

WIN A JONES SEWING MACHINE—guess the value of a dress literally made of money—lots of money! (First Floor).

WIN A JONES KNITTING MACHINE—guess how much wool was used to knit a certain garment. (First Floor)

PATON & BALDWINS, in conjunction with Lewis's and the Birmingham Mail Housewives Circle—place 8 designs in order of fashion appeal and win £50. Other prizes too. (20th May).

CORGI SPOT-THE-MODEL COMPETITION for children up to 14 years. You could win up to £5 worth of Mettoy Playcraft Models. (Fifth Floor).

SPECIAL DISPLAYS AND DEMONSTRATIONS

by many leading manufacturers covering a wide field of merchandise for men, women, children and the home. Many of the Cosmetic Houses are offering exciting free gifts with purchases of their goods.

Retired employees at their monthly get-together, c. 1975.

Staff, connected with Goods Inward and Pre-retailing Departments,
mark the retirement of Ernest Bates (centre), April 1981.

The fabric and patterns department three days before the final closure.

ACKNOWLEDGEMENTS
(for providing photographs, for encouragement and numerous other favours)

Ron Allso; The late Stanley Arnold; José Austell; Barbara Ball; Christine Barlow; Dennis Barlow; Bee Cee Enterprises; Norman Bettney; Birmingham City Council, Dept. of Economic Development; Birmingham City Council, Dept. of Planning and Architecture; Birmingham International Airport plc; Birmingham Post & Mail Ltd.; Nell Blackburn; Pauline Boyett; Colin Bragg; Cadbury Ltd.; Dave Carpenter; John and Chris Clayton; Joan Collier; Currie & Warner Ltd.; Arthur Deeley; Ivy and Des Done; Fred Dorrell; Eddystone Radio Ltd.; Val Ellson; Margery Elvins; David Everitt; Jean Fletcher; Judith Foster; Eric and Pat Giles; Peter Gupwell; Brian and Val Hastings; Lottie Hood; Anne Jennings; Dave and Thelma Jones; Lyn and Christine Jones; Kalamazoo plc; Norman Kilgour; Olive Leaman; Leyland DAF Vans Ltd.; Simon Livingstone; Maisie Mills; Dennis Moore; Edward Morgan; Peter Moss; John O'Keefe; Linda Park; The Patrick Collection; Gordon Peters; John Pinnick; Geoff and Linda Price; RAC Motoring Services; Eric and Dorothy Reeves; William Sapcote & Sons Ltd.; Joyce Scott; Keith Shakespeare; Cynthia Shayler; Mike Sheehan; Colin and Val Smith; W. H. Smith & Son Ltd, Moseley; Brian Spate; Phil Teague; Jill Treadwell; Jean Vaughan; Andy Wade; Tim Walton; Joan Wanty; Christina White; Bob and Joan Wilkes; Robert Wilkes; Rosemary Wilkes; Brenda Wilshaw.

Please forgive any possible omissions. Every effort has been made to include all organisations and individuals involved in the book.

Back Cover:

Jamaica Row, 30th December 1960.

The work force of Leyland DAF celebrate with David Duggins (left) representing the Receivers and Managing Director, Allan Amey, the employee/management buy-out, Common Lane, Washwood Heath, 26th April 1993.